Michael,
Thank you for support
and I hope you enjoy the
read. Much Love ♡

Welcome!

Day in and day out of my life in the mortuary world. Personal feelings, thoughts, and experiences. Emotions are high in this realm of life and hopefully I can move your thoughts to higher vibrations while leveling you out when it comes to transitioning into a "New Life".

Come along!

UNDERTAK<u>HER</u>

MEMOIRS OF A MORTICIAN

JANAE' L. KEARSE

UNDERTAK<u>HER</u>
MEMOIRS OF A MORTICIAN

The events and conversations in this book have been written with some names and details intentionally omitted to protect the privacy of individuals and their families.

Copyright © 2021 by Janae' L. Kearse

ISBN: 978-1-300-15420-4

Printed in the United States of America

www.jlkearse.com

This is a dedication to my grandmother, the Late Celia Mae Walker, who lit the flame of curiosity in my Mortuary Science world.
You are truly missed Grandma.

To my mother, father, and brother who love to listen to my "Funeral Home Daily" happenings.
You are appreciated.

To Granda, for showing me what it means to love unconditionally, through sickness and health.

To my friends who love the fact I can stomach in one day what they wish to never experience in a life time. Y'all are awesome.

To myself, for digging deep and pushing to perfect my craft.
Keep working lady.

I love you all; so deep.

CHAPTER 1

THE INFAMOUS QUESTION

"What made you want to do that?"

Simply put, on a busy day or a day when I am coasting through and keeping it all together while everything is falling apart, I would respond: "I don't really have an answer to that question".

After a gazillion times of getting this question and realizing how interested one can be in what I do, I analyzed and assessed a little more. Hmm…

So … here I am, five years into my journey as a mortician, sharing the REAL behind why I am here. Whew!

In October of 2000, it had been a normal day until night fell. Grandma wasn't feeling well and ended up going to the hospital. Daddy stayed home with my brother and I while mommy went to accompany Granda at the hospital. This moment I literally remember as if it were just yesterday when these events took place. It often times sucks to recall every moment so vividly, but I love every precious memory down to the last.

Mommy called back to let us know they could not do anything for Grandma in my hometown so she would need to be airlifted to a city nearby to be diagnosed and to receive proper treatment for what was going on. Grandma previously had open heart surgery years back and she had also never been in any type of aircraft before this particular night. The doctors said her heart was extremely weak upon arriving at their facility and the flight had her anxiety out of the roof. The doctors ran tests, did x-rays and immediately found out what was going on with Grandma but it was simply too late. She was too weak for surgery and it was nothing else they could do to help her.

Grandma took her first and last flight on October 30, 2000, and even though her shell landed in the hospital her soul went on to meet her maker. Her forever resting place. No more baggage. No more pain. She fought a good fight.

At the age of 10, I had experienced my first death that of course hit close to home; IT WAS HOME!

In the car the next day, Wyclef Jean's song "911" came on in the car and normally I would sing-along in the car but this day was different. Even though he obviously wasn't talking about his grandmother passing in the song, the words hit my heart a little differently at that moment.

cues music "If death comes for me tonight girl, I want you to know that I love you… Someone please call 9-1-1, tell them I just been shot down and bullet's in my heart; and it's piercing through my soul, feel my body getting cold."

sigh You get my drift. That song was heavy that particular day and even now as an adult it takes me back to that very moment. Grandma had not been shot and she went out peacefully but the reference to the heart and soul that he described was one of my very own. I felt like a piece of my heart and soul left me.

Days went by and family gathered at Granda's house and I sat in my room at his house as I normally would; sometimes alone, other times talking to my cousins. The family began to get worried because they felt like I wasn't doing well with processing what was going on. They asked my parents if I was ok and if I was talking about how I was feeling. I did not cry often; I was sad but no one could tell; I didn't say much but that was pretty normal for me. But, all was well.

Grandma had been gone in the physical but she came back to me every night and it kept me going. School had gotten hard in a sense of trying to focus and my grades shifted a little during this period of grieving but nothing too major because she stayed by my side. She would talk to me at night and it seemed as if she were really there in my room with me. Some would say it was her spirit, others would consider it dreaming because we were really close and I was missing her. I did not want to and honestly did not care to dig deeper into the situation because all I needed to know was that she was there for me. I processed her death and grieved on my own time and in my own way.

Usually when a loved one passes away, we are able to see them one last time, if we're "lucky", then they go away, and we do not see them until it's time for the service but...

WHAT HAPPENS DURING THE HOURS IN BETWEEN?!?!?

That, in fact, became MY question. Everyday, I wanted to know where they took Grandma. What are they doing to her? What is she doing? Does she have clothes on? When will we get to see her?

In a family with a funeral home, it would be normal to see all of these things, but I am a first generation mortician in my family and even though these questions were asked, most went UNANSWERED. No pressure there though, I understood those weren't "normal" questions for the outsiders.

I graduated from high school, went on to play collegiate sports and earned a Bachelor's degree in History, and I STILL had this curiosity of what goes on behind the doors of a funeral home/mortuary.

I applied to mortuary school, got accepted to mortuary school, prepared to go to mortuary school, and packed my things and off I went to MORTUARY SCHOOL. Finally, 13 years of wondering what, when, where, who, and how and now I can finally get the answers I've always wanted.

This, is what made me want to do this, as the people say.

Grandma made me want to do this!

July 22

Closer 2 U

Never rode on a plane before... July 22...
First time ever. I'm overjoyed, happy, excited,
nervous, scared, and last but certainly not least I'm

Closer 2 U

Sleepover with Daddy. Texts, phone calls, and words
filled with warmth coming from the ones I love.
But still there is no DEFINITE destination for me
right now as I'm thousands of miles in the air.
All that I am certain of is that I'm

Closer 2 U

Twenty years. One month. Four days.
That is all I can claim as mine as of today at
this very moment! Will I continue this exciting
journey in this crazy, cruel, hectic, loving, warm
thing we call life?? Who knows?
All that I know right now is I'm

Closer 2 U

I was told I have to be a "BIG GIRL" when experiencing
things such as what I'm experiencing right now...
This very moment. It's hard though. Not knowing
if I will ever breathe that lovely South Carolina
air that we used to share but we are truly
experiencing this excursion together and I truly
feel I'm

Closer 2 U

Waiting after being checked in, sitting with my daddy... Sharing laughs and more irreplaceable, enjoyable moments. I describe it as the BEST FATHER-DAUGHTER relationship EVER and I know our bond is sincere and unbreakable no matter how many hard times we go through. I thought watching him watch me walk away was going to be easy but honestly it felt like one of the hardest things I've ever had to do!!! Tears filled my eyes as I realize that he is not beside me but I am making this trip by myself. And with that being said, still yet I'm...

Closer 2 U

Sitting here listening to my iPod, looking out of the window everything is so small and I feel like I'm on top of the world and just as I feel on a daily basis, NOBODY is above me! But yet I'm

Closer 2 U

I can't stop tears from filling my eyes for some reason but I just gave myself a good laugh! The lady came by to give me some gingerale that I asked for, she handed me the cup of ice and the can... But when I went to pour it it spilled all in my seat! HaHa! Now I'm gonna look like I wet my pants! I'm hoping it dries quick and I know you are laughing at me right now. It's just in us and it makes me know and realize I'm

Closer 2 U

At this high altitude gives me a feeling that I'm close to you like I'm being blessed with your presence all over again... Such a wonderful feeling! I've said a prayer for the fam and all of my loved ones and now I completely understand what happens before I reach Houston is out of my hands but I also know if something happens to me right now I wish to go no other place except...

Closer 2 U

Right now I feel like I'm at peace with no worries whatsoever and I can only imagine how you feel ?!? Must be nice and it may be an envious feeling coming over me but I know my day is coming. Sooner or later... I just rather it be later :) then I'll be

Closer 2 U

Watch over me. Guide me. Love me, Encourage me. Infuse wisdom, kindness, and strength throughout my body and know that I will forever be your baby girl. No matter how far we are from each other, you live inside of me, therefore I'm

Closer 2 U.   —Janae' Licinia Kearse

A poem written to Grandma Celia Mae on my first flight ever.

CHAPTER 2

DAILY MORNING ROUTINE

After a morning struggle of Atlanta's "lovely" traffic, I arrive at the workplace, ready to find out what's in store for the day. I can definitely promise you there are no two days alike around here.

I pull up hoping there's not anyone sitting in the parking lot before business hours waiting for me to get there. People really take this time when you get in the building for granted. I need that alone time to feel like I can properly start my day. I hate walking into chaos. My typical morning would be arriving to an empty parking lot, grabbing the newspaper, cutting on the lights and doing a quick walk through the building to make sure nobody is in the back playing around and they are all resting peacefully. I always chuckle at the thought of that really happening when I come in! After my walk through, I sit at the desk and read the newspaper. Yes, as ancient as it may sound I still read the newspaper. I'm pretty sure this comes from Granda always having a newspaper available. I don't watch television much but the newspaper definitely helps to keep me updated with current events. It's actually pretty wack to see it get smaller and smaller as the years go by. My daily readings are normally concluded once I read my horoscope and the funny pages which you may know as the comics. Newspaper comics are pretty funny, but I will admit it takes a special kind of humor to really enjoy a nice little giggle from them. If you get a chance, grab a newspaper and check the "funny pages" out. LOL! Thank me later!

My mind doesn't always stay focused on one thing so I often times find myself venturing off to explore what snapchat filters are available. Of course this only happens on slower work days but I must admit; I love playing with those filters. The funny faces, the voice changes, the face swap; these things really tickle my soul! Snapchat definitely gets more saved pictures than actual posts from me.

Social Media is fun but I also get bored with it quick so you know what that means. We're on to the next thing. Ever since I've been in Atlanta I've noticed the great number of homeless people or street walkers; whatever you would prefer to call them. Some are nice, some are pretty bitter and mean, and then some you can just never tell what kind of space they are in. Morning people watching in East Atlanta is so refreshing for me. It'll keep you grounded if you allow it to do so. Not grounded in a sense of being judgmental but I see it as grounded in a sense of not being uptight and living free and unapologetic. These individuals walk the streets everyday just "figuring it all out" as they go. Say what you want but I feel like there's a lesson for people to learn here. Of course the average person would talk down and say they don't deserve certain things because they are capable of going to get a job just like everyone else but, what if they can't? What if they aren't mentally stable enough to be put in such a controlled environment? What if they physically cannot manage being in a controlled environment? Even emotionally…What if they just cannot handle the everyday work environment. The reality of it is, if you're currently reading this book, it is not your reality and I think it should be left at just that. No matter their situation or the circumstance, they are managing the way they know how. Help them out or let them be. I've spoken with a few here and there and it's not necessarily what they want to do but they have acknowledged the fact that they can make more money in a day on the streets than they can by accepting a job that they absolutely hate, only making minimum wages. So now, who's the smart one here? Us for showing up to a confined space everyday for a set rate or the ones that hang out in the beautiful streets filled with fresh air all day racking up who knows how much money from any and everybody? Don't answer that, just think about it. I'm sure your mind goes straight to stability. And the thought of bad weather conditions and what if they don't make much money on any given day but honestly who cares? The bottom line is those people know how to survive; no questions asked. Who are we to judge? So I challenge you to change your mindset and every time you see someone holding a sign for change or food, even if you do not choose to help them out in a monetary way, help them out by sharing a smile or a wave. Remember they are people too. Living human beings, days may be rough, but they have feelings too.

My current fave to watch is my wheelchair walker. Sounds funny right? Well, let me tell you, to see it in person is hilarious. This guy has a group of friends up the street a good little ways that he hangs out with early in the mornings and when he's done he'll start walking towards the corner store with his wheelchair. What you learn about these infamous street walkers is that when they find an area they like, they hang around and you'll see them over and over again. So picture me watching this every single day. He walks past my window, walking fine, pushing the wheelchair and when he gets just about to the business sign, he fluffs the pillow on the wheelchair and sits down like he really needs it as he heads for the corner store. Absolutely hilarious to see and I bet he thinks no one knows his daily route to the corner store. I thank him for the unknown smile and giggles that he gives me every day.

Another one of my favs right now and she's actually a newbie. Somehow she applies new, different color makeup on her face everyday, has a shopping cart from Target and does not have much in it at all but I guess that's still better than carrying everything in your hands all day? It tickles me the most that she wears her panties on the outside of her jeans with not a care in the world. Now as I said before, some are nice, some are mean, and some are indifferent. She's definitely in the last category. She'll look at you but she will not say anything; will not bother you at all. I've actually never seen her talk to anyone but day by day she's still going. Her unique looks helps me spot her out every time with her pink makeup, or red with heavily blushed cheeks and pink hair. Everything is loud and over the top, but it's HER own look.

People watching is easily done in the morning when things are calm but is definitely an all day event. Some even stop by on super hot days to ask random questions but I really think they just stop by for some good cool air. A quick question and off they go.

Welp…snap out of it!!

Newspaper read, plants watered, people watching over; it's time to get to work. Let the day begin!

CHAPTER 3

JENNY

Who is Jenny you ask? Ok so maybe you didn't but ladies and gentlemen, I introduce to you...Jenny!

Jenny was once about a 5 pound block of wax and an empty plastic mannequin head. Actually she was more like a skeleton head. No eye shape, no nose, no lips, literally a skeleton head. Countless hours, much trial and error, and a whole lot of patience and "Jenny" arrived.

Jenny is a real life representation of one of my favorite parts of being a mortician. The restorative work. Tedious but very therapeutic. I know a lot of people shy away from this because it can take up so much time but I love, love, love seeing the before and after. Sickly, elderly, gun shot wound victims, improperly cared for individuals, no matter the situation I love working to get people's loved ones back to an image they like, can accept, and will forever remember.

Restorative work is my thing.
Give me time.

Watch me work!

The coolest thing to me going through Restorative Arts class in mortuary school was definitely the measurements of our facial features.

Generally speaking, the length of your ear is equal to the length of your nose and the width of your eye is equal to the distance between your eyes.

Yeah, I know you tried it. Cool huh?

The length of your face can be divided into three equal parts. Your ears fall in the middle third of your face. The mouth is two eyes wide. The face is approximately five eyes wide. Learned something?

*Fun fact: I do not and have not ever tried doing my own makeup but I can certainly make my clients look good!

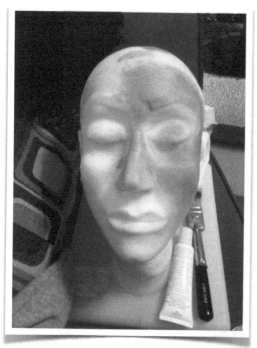

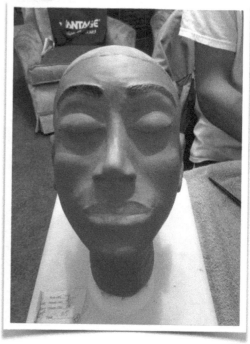

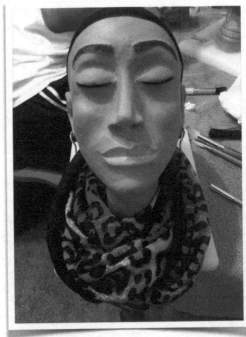

WHAT DO YOU THINK ABOUT JENNY?

CHAPTER 4

14 DAYS OF NAE'

Consider yourself in line for an emotional roller coaster of what I have personally felt and witnessed on 14 different days.

But consider this a radio edited version because listen…

I'll leave it at that.

Day 1

I take a vacation for a week with my parents every year and currently this is the first day back at work since vacation. Enough said already, right? Get me. One of the hardest things to do is to come back to work full force when you have literally been out living your best life without a care in the world. Unable to focus and still wanting to be on vacation just simply doing what you want to do without having specific tasks to get done. I could've had a few more days on the beach but of course, vacation is NEVER long enough.

* Fun Fact: Talk about a near "death" experience, I had the pleasure of being stung by a jellyfish while I was on vacation. YIKES! I immediately jumped when I felt something grabbing my elbow and as I looked at it I couldn't really see anything on my arm but it looked very gooey. Daddy asked what happened as if I was playing but this time I was serious. It was a natural reaction to rub my arm as I was trying to make it back to shore where Mommy was sunbathing and just as I said it looked, it felt thick and slimy; sticky. As I sat down, I didn't really know what to do so I started googling. "Can a jellyfish sting kill?" "What do you put on a jellyfish sting?" You know, all of the worst case scenarios pop up first. One specifically said, "Jellyfish are extremely venomous and can become fatal within two minutes". *sigh* Mommy was already concerned and

wanted to go to the room so I definitely did not share that with her but I did decide to ask the lifeguard if he had something for the sting because it had been a few minutes and my arm was still stinging very badly and it had begun to swell. He sprayed my arm and told me I would be fine and suggested using a warm compress when I got back in the room to help with the swelling. I monitored how I felt as I sat on the beach a little longer. Eventually we went back inside and after I showered, Mommy placed a warm towel on my arm and I was honestly amazed at how much it helped with the swelling. Thank goodness, I survived this attack.

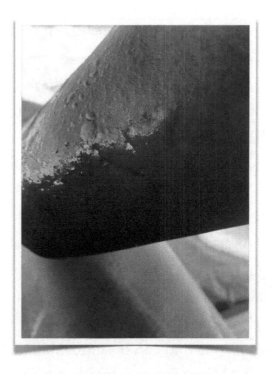

swollen jellyfish sting after getting it sprayed by life guard

Now, as I was saying vacation was finally over. I already received calls while I was away about tasks that needed to be done, how they should be done, and a few other issues that were going on. I try to leave work at work on most days for my own sanity but of course with me being out for a week I didn't mind answering a few questions here and there. As I sat at work today, everyone expressed how happy they were to see me and glad I was back. In my head, I'm like "Yes, because it's less work for you all to do now but I'm glad to have been missed."

I made arrangements for two families but they were surprisingly the easiest part of the day. Good families, and they pretty much knew exactly what they wanted. You can't really ask for anything more than that when dealing with clients in here.

Work was overwhelming today to be honest.

Unfortunately, I expected a lot to not be done while I was gone, aside from handling the services that were scheduled and making sure the families had everything they needed but files that I intentionally worked on before leaving were all out of order and in different places from where I left them. HEADACHE ALREADY! Not only did someone move the files that I had sorted and separated, they put ALL of the files together. (let's laugh instead of crying right now)

Yup, so you know what that means for me; DOUBLE WORK. I spent the day kinda sorta going through files and trying to figure out which ones I worked on already and which ones needed to be worked on but not for long. It just wasn't one of those days. I did a little here and there and tended to the folks that came in but I chose to coast through this day. It was needed. Better luck tomorrow. This became exhausting.

Day 2

A new day, picking up where I left off yesterday and certainly in a better space mentally to get things done. I hit the ground running when I arrived at work. Pulled all of the files out and immediately got to work. I was able to get all of the files in their own individual stacks and proceeded with what I was finalizing before I left. This day was going pretty good and I knew it would be a very productive day for me. This, was a day when I wish I could turn the phones off or have them forwarded to someone else while I get busy.

People were calling left and right about death certificates, cremains, prices, pre-arrangements, notary services, you name it. Just any and everything you could imagine, they were calling.

For my families, this has been a rough week and of course my heart goes out to each and everyone per usual, no matter the circumstance. A loss in a family is a loss. At this point, it's just Tuesday and I've had a family dealing with a homicide and a family dealing with a suicide. Wasn't much more to this day. Faxed more death certificates to doctors to be signed, had a few certified copies picked up from the vital records office, translated some paperwork that needed to go to Mexico and ended my day.

OFFICE BACK IN ORDER.

Day 3

I wasn't able to get much rest last night and I woke up with a slight headache. I usually never get headaches so when I do, its normally from a lack of sleep. I know that I need an ample amount of rest to properly function and when it gets thrown off, its uncomfortable.

A twenty to twenty-five minute drive to work easily weighed in at a strong hour this morning due to traffic. I literally drove about 14 mph, 93% of the way. Talk about a bummer.

I HATE TRAFFIC!

Even though I had a headache already this morning, I was still feeling really good and excited about finishing a few tasks from the day before. More doctor offices to call, more death certificates to process, cremation paperwork to get ready. But today was also a day in which the family was coming to identify their family member and say their final good byes before he went off to the crematory.

When a case goes to the medical examiner's office, we never really know how the corpse is going to arrive. Yesterday, the family of the homicide victim came in to make arrangements and were going to come back today to view their loved one. I get a call from the mother and she's concerned that she may not be able to see her son one last time because his face is possibly not viewable. I hate to hear that from the family because most of the time they do not know how any of these situations work and it freaks them out. I had to calm her down, hear what she was telling me the medical examiner's office shared with her and explain to her that I could not give her any answers to her questions until he arrives at the funeral home. I normally pray about these things in hopes of better findings when it comes to the state of the body.

I was relieved to see that his face was perfectly fine and they would be able to see him one last time. This was a large family and you could tell they were very close to each other.

You could feel the love, you could feel the hurt.

I called the man's mother back and told her what was considered good news in the midst of a bad situation and she was so shocked but I could hear the joy in her voice after being told she would be able to see her son ONE LAST TIME.

The family came and as I expected it was a parking lot full. The mother and one of her daughters walked in first and as I guided them in she looked at me with hurt in her eyes. I escorted her to her son and comforted her as she cried. After they made sure he was presentable for the other family members, I walked outside to get them. They came in and as each one of them walked in, the tears were flowing.

As they left the chapel and went back outside, the children stood in a circle with their mother with their arms stretched around the next to form a circle. I would like to consider this a CIRCLE OF LOVE. They cried and hugged but it was their moment to share. It was beautiful. They were there for each other. I can provide comfort but it's everything and more to me when a family can lean on each other. It reminds me of my family.

Today was a good day, very productive, and I have a much shorter stack of files from what I started with on Monday. It's hump day, and I am tired. I will sleep good tonight.

Day 4

As I sit here getting my hair braided, I let my idle mind wander and decide to have a moment of self reflection. A chance to analyze a situation and figure out things to come.

Today was one of those days that brings you back to reality and realize there's always room for improvement. A lady's husband took his life a few days ago and of course she hasn't been taking it well. She came in to view the chapel and also sign the authorization form for us to pick him up from the medical examiner's office.

I had not had much interaction with her before this aside from answering a few questions here and there but you can never underestimate the effect you have on someone. Daddy always says "You only get one chance to make a first impression" and in fact, a first impression is a lasting impression no matter how much a person changes.

I had spoken to someone that knows the lady and through this person being transparent and knowing me, she shared some "off the record" information with me. Apparently her friend had been considering switching funeral homes because she didn't feel as much empathy and compassion as she felt she needed at the moment. Her mannerisms seemed to be fine when she came in and even though we can't do much if a person isn't giving us any feedback or making it known what they need, I still hate to feel like I'm not enough for any of my families that I serve. Part of my role here is to comfort and console during these hard times and I try my best to hold myself to doing that in the best way possible; every time.

I say this to say, always appreciate constructive criticism. The lady said I was unprofessional but her friend assured her that I am very professional when it comes to my work but I also needed to completely understand what she needed from us. She was able to speak with her friend and see what was going on to help her move forward with the process and to finalize plans. I hate that she felt that way especially during this time, however I'm glad she has decided to stay.

After I got off today I decided to check on one of my childhood friends and see how he was doing. Him and his lady friend are expecting a child so I like to check in; babies are special.

Day 5

Today was a normal work day but as urns, flowers, regular mail, and pretty much any deliveries come to the funeral home you see the different reactions of people. So many of them are scared to come inside or don't want to walk past the front door and sometimes they even come in looking from side to side like someone is going to jump out at them.

PURE COMEDY, OK!!

We have this one young lady that works for UPS, the sweetest young lady ever and probably the most consistent in my years of being here. I think aside from me being there to greet her and always allowing her to leave packages at the front, I am like 97% sure the funeral home is her least favorite stop. I've been here for over five years now and she has consistently been bringing packages over the years and nothing has changed. She DOES NOT want to know or discuss anything beyond the front door. To be honest, she doesn't even like to think about what she is delivering in the boxes that she drops off. One day she was coming in, bringing a box that was large enough for a human to actually fit in it and I met her at the door. I looked at her, ready to drop the box off and asked, "Is he heavy?"

Listen…
The funniest thing ever!
She instantly looked spooked like she saw a ghost run by in front of her. She took her hands off of the huge box like she

could feel someone in the box and then took a moment to simply think and realize that no person would really be shipped that way and had to laugh at herself. You just have to appreciate folks catching on and loving a little humor in the middle of a busy work day. Besides, most people think funeral homes are scary and the people are uptight and stoic.

BLAH!

From that day on it was almost like she found a new confidence about herself bringing those packages in. She still doesn't waste any time getting in and getting out but I'm pretty sure she knows nothing is in those boxes that she's delivering is going to jump out and grab her!

Day 6

Well.. I would really like to give you something good, but today was just one of those quiet work days. The phone did not ring until three hours after I arrived at work. Nobody has been in to see me, ask questions, or make a payment for anything at this point either.

Now some may complain about these kind of work days but I don't mind being the first to say I thoroughly enjoy these days every blue moon; it gives you a chance to breathe and focus on more paperwork in the office versus having to speak with someone every second of the day. I believe we are so used to constantly doing things at work, even if it's just a desk job, that we forget how draining it is to talk to people all day. We all need a break. I prefer having one mid-day instead of going full force all day and then crashing at the end of the day because my brain has been overloaded.

Oh yeah, that call that finally came after being at work for three hours…

It definitely turned into an hour and a half counseling session. A nice lady called and simply needed to vent about her family. She fussed, shed a few tears, laughed, and thanked me for being so kind to her as she went on her rant about her "dysfunctional family". It's all love.

"I am glad I could be a listening ear and of some assistance to you today."

Day 7

On this day, I would like to push you to know, recognize, and understand the dangers of STRESS!

We've been dealing with a young lady trying to handle funeral arrangements for her father over the past few weeks and it was really an unfortunate situation for her. She was not only dealing with him being gone but has also had to deal with his girlfriend and one of her sisters trying to go against every decision she has made.

The daughter that we have been dealing with said her father always wanted to come to our funeral home when he passed away so she wanted to honor his wishes of dealing with a funeral home that has handled services for many other family members. After getting him here, she realized the insurance policy was shared with her sister that wanted him to go to a different funeral home. After a short battle of deciding if she can afford to keep him with us and make payments alone, or if she needed to send him to the other funeral home; she allowed them to take him to the other establishment and plan the funeral so the insurance could cover it.

Simple, right?

WRONG!

So her sister and the girlfriend of her father went to the other funeral home, planned the service, and had the service but…

THEY DID NOT PAY ANY CEMETERY FEES FOR HIM TO BE BURIED!

The young lady called, hysterically crying and asking for advice and help with what she should do next. Her father's service had been held over the weekend at this point and it was starting a new week of him being back at the funeral home with no plans in motion for him to be buried. I told her to talk to them even though she did not want to because they had the insurance information and that they could just sign and agree to let the money for the cemetery be taken out of that and she ended the phone conversation that day saying she would try to reach out to them and get them to do that.

Speaking with her a few days later, they still did not have it figured out. Apparently they had no intentions of spending anymore money to bury their father and told her sister she would have to figure it out.

Long story short, I gave her a price for us to pick her father up and take him to the cemetery to be buried. She was able to come up with the money and about a week later we were able to bury him. I could see, hear and feel all of her emotions.

She was sad.
She was hurt.
She was exhausted.

She was STRESSED!

This young lady expressed to me on the phone how stressful this entire situation had been on top of her losing her father.

Well... I had her father's death certificate ready that following week and called her to pick it up. To my surprise, a family member explained to me that this same lady's funeral service was going to be taking place on the following Saturday. Things with her father had gotten that heavy. This was so sad to hear. Stress escorted her right to her death bed.

Day 8

Today was one of those days when I feel like I am not being respected in the best way because I am not the wanted voice on the other side of the phone.

This guy is older and he normally deals with the owner of the funeral home but the owner no longer handles the daily operations and hasn't been since I've been here. Of course, you try to explain this but it goes in one ear and out of the other. I even tried to tell him I can help him, but he is convinced he needs to speak with the owner because that's who he normally speaks with. Well sir, I hate to inform you but the owner WILL NOT be coming to the phone today. He is not here and he only comes in when he wants to. Even if you were able to speak with him, he's just going to refer you right back to Janae' to get the help you need. That's why I am here at this point; to keep them from having to do this work.

After speaking with him for a while, I finally reached a point where he is convinced that I can help him with what is going on. I understand these times are sensitive and people can be very emotional so no matter how I feel on a particular day about whatever may be going on, I still have to address families accordingly. This is probably when my patience is tested the most; when they are not able to speak with who they think can help them out the most.

Man... it's tough.

After coming to a common ground about what's going on and why he only wants to speak with the manager, he really did not have a reason. It was really just one of those situations where he's an older gentleman and we all know most older folks prefer to deal with who they would normally deal with. He finally said "Well, yea I guess it is about time for him to pass the work on and relax after all of these years." Ha.

"Yes, Yes it is, sir."

He tells me his son has passed away and we figure out a time for him to come in and make arrangements and end the phone conversation on a good note that day. I will see him when he comes in; I am the only one here to assist him at the moment.

Fast forward to him coming in…

He is an older guy, as I expected. I also expected him to come in pretty grumpy and with an attitude but I greeted him with a warm smile and a little joke followed by, "Come on in here and let me help you!"
Older folks love a little joke.
We sit down, we talk, we discuss what he wants. TUH. I get the job done! As I knew I would. He was pleased with the services that were set to take place and was well on his way to grieve the loss of his son. Before he left though, he thanked me for helping him and told me he was happy he was able to meet with me. He admitted he gave me a hard time on the phone and apologized. I wasn't looking for that but it feels good to hear that from him because this happens more often

than you could even imagine but very rarely with an apology to follow.

He commended me on how well I handled him on the phone and in-person and went on to say how professional I was. He appreciated my patience. In these cases though, when someone expresses their gratitude for my patience I always make sure I let them know I appreciate their patience too and their willingness to allow me to help them during this tough time.

My difficult clients. You just gotta love them. And we ALWAYS part ways on a good note.

To this very day, when he comes in the funeral home he has the sweetest, most gentle attitude with me and he has even offered to buy me lunch. I'll always remember him and I am sure he'll always remember me.

Day 9

Broken Heart Syndrome... It's real.

Do you believe in broken hearts?
Do you see it ONLY as a figure of speech?
Is it really a thing?

On this day, it was a moment of sadness that passed through my mind, body, and soul as two daughters of a mother that we buried last year came in to now make final arrangements for their father.

Their mother passed away in January of last year; now their father is gone. They said he wasn't sick or feeling bad, he had just not been the same since his wife passed. This was a simple family, these two sisters had literally just gone through this process and they made it known they wanted the same thing for their father that we had done for their mother.

Their parents were gone, but they had each other and you can certainly tell they were leaning on each other for support. We were able to handle business, laugh, joke, and lift the mood a little each day they came in.

When it came time for them to do their family viewing they continued to let their personalities and relationship with their father show.

Youngest Daughter: Aww... he has a pleasant smile on his face, he looks really good.

Oldest Daughter: Daddy you play too much!

Youngest Daughter: OOOO he just looks so good, take me and my daddy's picture.

I love it! There's nothing like that Daddy-Daughter bond and it's refreshing to witness one outside of my own.
So, back to my question…
Do you believe in broken hearts?

No, technically the death certificate is not going to list the cause of death as a broken heart but families can witness the change in their family member after being happily married to someone for 30, 40, 50, and 60 plus years and then all of a sudden having to learn how to live without them. I'm sure it's painful and probably the saddest part of marriage; in my mind.
These girls felt like their father simply passed from A BROKEN HEART and that served as their comfort.

Day 10

Today I went to a client's house so she could sign some papers without going through the hassle of finding someone to bring her to the funeral home. I called her when I came to work to see if that would be better for her and she quickly agreed that it would be a great way to get that done.

When I pulled up to the house I called to let her know I was outside and she came to the door to greet me. She had the cutest little dog and was so sweet per usual. Her house was quiet and she put her four legged baby in another room so he would not be in the way. I have fur babies of my own so I quickly let her know, I did not mind her dog being out because I did not want him to cry the entire time wondering if his human was ok out here with this stranger. If you have a fur baby, you know they can be protective; no matter how big or small.

As we started getting the paperwork completed, she started mentioning how different it is without her brother there and even the dog knows and feels that he is not there. He sits in his chair, walks in the room to look for him, goes outside for what would've been their normal routine and then comes back in. I'm pretty sure my thoughts are a bit biased but do we really deserve the love our dogs give us? I mean, the perfect example of unconditional love. We can fuss at them when they are wrong but they are still going to come right back to love on you.

We must've sat and talked for hours, sharing story after story and it was just a beautiful moment. Moments I live for in this profession, to simply lift someone's spirits by just offering them some time out of my day. She misses her brother and admits the house will never be the same again but she knows she has done all she could do for him. Her stories, even with such an age gap, were relatable. Before I left we were able to share one more laugh as her and her precious little dog walked me outside. She said she was going to give him a treat for behaving so well but, SHE SPELLED IT OUT! Y'all I was so shocked and so happy. They know the word treat so well that whenever they hear it they expect one. Me and Mommy have to say T-R-E-A-T when talking around the pups so they don't get excited and she literally had to do the same thing. Man I tell you what, this visit was not just for her but it also blessed my spirit for the day. Laughs that were definitely needed and a clear space to provide an ear.

As I walked to my car she continuously thanked me for bringing the papers to her to be signed but more importantly she thanked me for giving her some good company during this time.

The feeling here has been mutual. I appreciated her opening up to me just as much and allowing herself to begin healing and grieving her brother's death.

Day 11

Not much to say here at all.

Today we have picked up our first coronavirus case. He was actually the first person in Georgia to pass from the virus; March 12, 2020.

I don't know how to feel right now. I did not really expect this to not happen but I certainly did not want it to happen either. I don't know if I want to even deal with this at the moment. Am I putting myself in danger? Is my family at risk? Will they be ok with this? Will sick families be coming into the office?

Sheesh.

It's just a lot to take in right now.

*Update: After doing some post mortem tests, it is actually believed that someone passed from COVID-19 before this March 12, 2020 death that was knowingly from COVID-19.

Day 12

Not much happened today but something very interesting happened today. On my "lunch break" I ran down the street to pick up a few things I needed. As I'm about to pull back up to work, I see these two people tussling on the ground. My first thought was, "Oh goodness, some East Atlanta folks back at it again" but then I realized it was actually a man and a woman and at this point they have an entire audience. Everyone is looking but no one decided to help because as I discussed in the previous chapter the two people were homeless. Most people's thought of homeless people is one of fear so they record instead of responding as if they weren't "normal people". Ugh!

Anyway, we stopped the vehicle and got out to see what's going on. I noticed the man and woman that are tussling are actually a couple that is normally walking down the street together; he would be on his bike, riding slow enough for her to walk right beside him at a nice pace.

Woman: Ma'am!! Please help me, please help me!

Man: Call the police! This is a citizen's arrest!

Y'all, I just couldn't even hold it together. I'm like now what in the world have you two gotten into today to act this way.

Woman: Ma'am, I'm just trying to go but he won't let me get up!

Man: Nope, I'm tired of you abusing me! You ain't going nowhere until the police come! Ma'am she threw a brick at my head and I'm tired of her doing this!

Tired of abuse and getting a brick thrown at you? Why not just leave her alone right? Easier said than done, CLEARLY!

We call the police and let them know they are on the way. I walk into the funeral home to go on with my day and shortly after the police came down the street, looking for the exact location of where the call was from. I walked back outside to make sure they were still there and you wouldn't believe what happened! These two were no longer tussling but sitting calmly, like there was never a problem! Haha! Crazy! The lady saw the police and decided she wanted to get up and the guy tackled her once again to continue his citizen's arrest and being adamant about her not leaving without them having a talk with her.

Pure comedy for them to snap in and out of that scene so quickly. I didn't hang around to see what happened. I figured the police officers would do their job and figure out what needed to be done, if anything at all.

The anxious, ready to record bystanders really grind my gears! Like the first thought nowadays is not to genuinely seek help for someone but instead it's "oh, let me get my phone out and record." Dang, can you at least record and help simultaneously or something?! Yea, thank you. Thank you so very much for ABSOLUTELY NOTHING!

Day 13

A lot has transpired on this particular day. I've had one of those "difficult" families that is not exactly on the same page. I have a daughter that doesn't necessarily hate her father but I can tell their relationship wasn't the best but I can also tell she has love for him. Now as her father's only child she is having to handle his funeral arrangements as his next of kin.

This is her first time. She is concerned. She is lost. She is uncertain. But…she is very open to allowing me to help her through this process. She is from up north and will be here until she handles the final arrangements for her father. She has gone through her father's house to see if he has insurance or anything that states what he would like his final method of disposition to be. To her surprise her dad left her a note in his insurance booklet from when she signed the policy years ago listing her as the beneficiary. She cried; she spoke her truth, she cleared her chest and I was glad a weight had been lifted off her shoulders.

The next day she came back so we could call the insurance company and make sure the policy was in good standing and was active to be used to pay for the services that were to be rendered for her father. Well…here comes another boulder falling off the side of the cliff to see if she's going to get knocked off or if she'll be able to dodge it. The insurance policy was no longer active. What she and I had both thought was figured out was now an unsolved problem; AGAIN. As her eyes began to swell with tears that she was trying to hold back, she asked "What am I going to do?" I believe we are all capable of figuring things out when we need to. Sometimes it takes a few deep breaths, a little more patience, and a clear thinking space. I advised her to take the rest of the day to get herself together and first deal with her father being gone, and talked about her forgiving him and herself for the years of no communication. She thanked me for my kindness, patience, and helpful words. I'm grateful but this is literally what I am here for. So thank you for allowing me to do my job.

In the midst of everything going on with this lady in the past few days that I've seen her, she called me this morning before arriving for her appointment. I'm thinking she needs to reschedule or has additional questions, but…she called to ask me if I wanted any coffee this morning!! WOW; just WOW! Now as you're reading this you may think, "Ok, a cup of coffee, so what?" but what I want you to understand is this woman just lost her father, doesn't have any good insurance to work with, doesn't live down here to know her way around and has to figure out this entire situation but she thought about ME! That's big to me and at that point; I knew I touched her in the slightest bit. That makes me happy to know that she knows I care and genuinely want to see her make it through this without having a breakdown. The day of the viewing she said she was thinking of writing her father a letter. I'm a paper and pen type of girl so I was all for it. "Whatever it is you need to get out; let him know. Free your mind, heart, and soul and pray for comfort in knowing that your father's soul is also at peace."

Day 14

Random lady came by today and asked if she and a few of her friends could park outside while they had their "Girls Day" in the area. She said they are all in their 80's; the cutest little ladies. She offered to pay me to park outside but I told her it was fine and she did not have to pay any fee. She said thank you and walked off with one of her friends. I go on to finish what I'm working on and here she comes walking back in! She has a plate in her hand and she's asking me if I like cake! LOL! She goes on to talk about how her best friend makes the best cakes and she wanted me to have her piece for being so kind to her and her girls. It's really awesome to come across genuinely nice people nowadays. It's refreshing; a breath of fresh air.

A family of one of the deceased individuals came in this morning to drop off some clothes for his brother. His brother had some personal items so he wanted to pick those up to see if a set of keys were there. Unfortunately, I didn't think the keys were there but he was so happy to still be able to have his brother's belongings. Before he left, he stopped and looked at me… At this point, I'm like uh oh; please don't tell me something is wrong! Something being wrong in here is WHEW! Fortunately, he took a deep breath, smiled, and said thank you and he appreciated all that we had done for his family.

CHAPTER 5

CHILDREN AND DEATH

What are you afraid of?

As adults, we tend to always want to "do what's best" for children. In the death and dying world, my question would be: "What is the best thing to do for children when a loved one has passed?" Do you stop them from showing emotions as they come to them? Do you allow them to make decisions about what they want to see and how much they can take at that particular time? What would you personally do?

Through my experience in the years I have been in the funeral service industry, it has normally been a decision made by the parent or guardian and not much of the child being able to speak for themselves.

To be honest, I completely disagree with this way of life when dealing with death.

As stated earlier, my interest in the funeral industry sparked from my grandmother passing away before I was a teenager. Ten years old, to be exact. From the time my grandmother passed to the time she was lowered into the ground, I was free to express my feelings and make my own decision based off of those same feelings. I knew Grandma was no longer with us, but I wanted to see her, I wanted to ask questions, I wanted to know that she was being taken care of.

Families come in the funeral home and I hear them telling other family members stories about letting their children know he or she is "sleeping". I'm not sure why, how, or where this initially came from but I see it as a form of fear. Who's afraid though? You as a parent or the child? The answer here lies in the fact that we try to think of what children may see after seeing a dead body. In movies, we see children viewing dead bodies and going into deep, dark spaces where they would be placed having nightmares about whoever they have seen.

Aside from telling children someone is sleeping, they will just cut them off completely and will not let them see their loved one. I can not begin to imagine how I would feel now as an adult if my parents had not let me see Grandma one last time before she was "taken away" from me forever. Someone so precious and so vital in my everyday life; a whole piece of my world.

Children have feelings. Children are human. Children have emotions. Children are real. Children know love. Children are FEARLESS... until...

FEAR IS INTRODUCED!

This is me, encouraging you to allow your children and children in general to deal with death exactly how you have to take it; head on. Allow them to feel, be open to talking to them and telling them the truth. Knowledge in every aspect of life is important. Death is the one thing that is for sure guaranteed.

CHAPTER 6

REGRETS AND COPING

Regret: sorrow aroused by circumstances beyond one's control or power to repair

Cope: to deal with and attempt to overcome problems and difficulties

As people, we have selfish ways. We tend to lean more towards what helps us or what is beneficial and aligned with what we have going on in our personal lives at any particular time. We favor ourselves and whatever is working for us during each season. Some of us see others as a burden when they have fallen ill and some just do not care what the next person may be dealing with.

In the funeral home, I have seen families come together like the toughest glue you can find on the market and I have seen others argue every second they are in the room making arrangements for their family member. I have seen people cry and lean on each other and I have seen some curse each other out until they are ready to fight in my office. Believe it or not, I have seen and witnessed a "visitation" where not one single person showed up to see this guy. Now what kind of life could someone possibly have lived that lead to ABSOLUTELY NO ONE coming to pay their respects to them when they passed away. Where is your family? What has happened over the years? Where's the forgiveness? Sheesh.

It's sad.

It's unfortunate.

It's real.

When families come in during what is normally the toughest journey they've had to face in their lives; losing mothers, fathers, brothers, sisters, and much more, emotions are high. But... there's a huge difference in emotions being high because you're sad and missing your loved one, and emotions being high because you know you could've done more and better by that particular loved one while they were here on this earth.

Most of the time when families come in and are not on the same page with everyone, there's normally a guilty conscience in the room. There's someone that knows they could have and should have done more for the person before they passed, away, but they never made time. This is usually the person that wants to take over and is seen as the one that is doing too much. Mama could've been the most simple, discreet, and the sweetest little lady but now this particular sibling wants to spend an unnecessary amount of money and wants everything to be fly and flashy. Not realizing, none of this is symbolic or shows the character of their mother, but only what they want to do to make things looks better and to say they did something for her. The reality of it is though, IT'S TOO LATE! Get over yourself. Do better by the ones that are still here on earth to be loved on. Get right with yourself; realize and learn from that previous mistake. As cliche as it may be, "Give people their flowers while they can actually smell them".

You do not want to find yourself living with regrets and figuring out a way to cope with the things that you never did for special people in your life forever. It will not be a good life for you to live. If this speaks to you, start now.

Start fresh, you are capable of having a clean slate at any point.

On the other side of this, family members that know what they want or what the deceased person wants, are obviously not afraid of the conversation. They wanted to make sure they knew what their loved one wanted for their final disposition and also carried it out. Now this is not necessary for everyone because we all know accidents happen as well as unexpected deaths. This is for the individuals that are watching someone's health fail them, or watching someone growing old, knowing that no matter how much we want to; we cannot keep them here forever. They feel like they are doing their part by being proactive. Being proactive in a sense of speaking on the next step of transitioning is not going to speed that process up at all. It's a conversation that needs to be had. Kind of like the old folks that always felt like the "Birds and the Bees" conversation was necessary.

It's all proper preparation.

These people are not living with regrets and they can properly cope and grieve the death of their loved one without a bunch of baggage hanging over their heads.

We all should strive to feel this way. The hurt is going to hurt. Days will be hard but doing your part when you can will help you tremendously. Still living, but the reassurance of telling yourself "job well done" is a true peace of mind.

Truly underestimated.

CHAPTER 7

MAKING FUNERAL ARRANGEMENTS

First things first, I am begging you right now. Please, please, please make an appointment with your funeral home of choice.

We do not mind helping you as a walk-in but it is so much more organized and convenient for you and your funeral director when an appointment is made. If you cannot make your appointment, call and reschedule; there are other families that also need to be helped. As funeral directors, we have to understand no two families will be the same and should be treated as such, but as clients we also have to learn to give that same courtesy and understand we are not the only ones with family members passing away. You cannot go to your funeral home of choice with an unruly attitude expecting to be seen when you want to be seen and not being caring towards other families during their moments of bereavement.

Making funeral arrangements for our loved ones is and will always be one of the hardest tasks we have to complete in life. It should be considered a blessing if you make it through your own life without having to ever step into the role of

NEXT OF KIN aka DECISION MAKER. It's a hard bed to lie in but it's rewarding to know you've had the chance to choose the final disposition in a way that would honor that particular loved one.

HOWEVER...

Once you step into the role of decision maker, let the first decision made be; who do I NEED to come with me to make the final arrangements? Susie Jane may be able to give me some input and be a good listener for me during this hard time just in case I miss something important, but do I really need Ralph here too?

I say this to say, when preparing to go to the funeral home for your appointment, take whoever you need to help you make the final decisions. Be respectful of the funeral home and other families and do not bring a million family members along for moral support. Ask them to wait for you at the family house to share the details of the services. When there are too many people, too many opinions, and one person in charge financially; decisions get harder to make. It causes tension amongst family members and can also cause a permanent separation between family members. It would be beneficial to you and it would cut back on some confusion.

CHAPTER 8

PRE-ARRANGEMENTS
VS
LIFE INSURANCE

Disclaimer: This chapter is not to discredit or take away from any insurance agent. This is solely based off of my personal experiences and what I have seen.

With that being said, the people need to know!

A big no-no I see due to the lack of knowledge is families having to raise money through a Go FundMe, a fish fry, or outright asking family and friends for money when the insurance policy falls through. Many people are definitely into just signing paperwork without reading it in its entirety. Yes, I too have been guilty of this but I read thoroughly now to clarify for myself and often times for others. Most of the time when getting insurance, we get the Whole Life policy, but the premium stays the same even as you age; the face value is paid to the beneficiary. However, most people sign and leave the insurance agent, ignorant to the fact that the policy has to be in effect for 2 years before the designated beneficiary is eligible to receive full benefits.

So basically what I'm saying here is if you start a new, Whole Life insurance policy today, you'll need to live at least two more years in order for your family to have that money to pay for your funeral expenses, or even for it to be left to your beneficiaries. If it falls shy of that two year mark, welp, premiums can be returned, but that's not going to be anything close to the 15K face value that you signed for, thinking it would be paid out in that amount immediately. A real life bummer, and I've witnessed someone pass a little over a month shy of the two year mark and the insurance company still considered the policy "contestable". When a policy is considered "contestable" it means the insurance company is not going to take on the responsibility of saying they will be fulfilling an assignment for the funeral home, in the amount of the funeral expenses. It's ineligible for full payout until they do an investigation to make a decision based off of medical records, etc. At this point, the leg work and headache for the family begins. They now have to fill out paperwork to send to the insurance company to try to get as much money out of the policy as possible while continuing to follow up to make sure it isn't just pushed to the side. They still have a funeral to plan and pay for, as well as time to properly grieve. It's a lot and it gets heavy. It's like driving home after working long hours on a foggy, rainy type of day, where you cannot see past your front bumper and then hitting something that leaves you on the side of the road with a flat tire. Everything seems to be going wrong at this point and the mind begins to spiral. Why me? What do I do now? Why is this happening to me? Many love to say, "Well they didn't tell me this when I started the policy. They said it will pay the full amount."

No, they probably did not tell you the specifics that were on the contract for you to read yourself, I agree.

Yes, it will pay out the full amount; if you live at least two more years.

I am not saying its right or fair but that's just the way it is. They are quick to receive your monthly premiums and quick to let you know your policy is about to lapse or has lapsed, but if everything is not in order when it comes time to pay the policy it will definitely be delayed.

There's nothing we can do about it at this point aside from advising you to share information with others about reading the details of a new insurance policy before signing the dotted line, and of course making sure you never make the same mistake again yourself.

For future references, I would like to recommend a solution to preventing this problem. If you have reached a certain age, have any terminal illness, have underlying health issues or any other concerns that may cause your insurance premiums to be really high or if you have been deemed uninsurable, go to your local funeral home of choice and make pre-arrangements.

Now… before you go through a whole spiel in your head about not wanting to plan your own death, don't even begin to think about it in that way.

Pre-arrangements are simply good pre-planning. You don't have a birthday party without pre-planning. You don't have a wedding without pre-planning. Look at this in the same light. Why have a funeral without planning and choosing your perfect ending? Not up to anyone else, just YOU. Now if your family does not honor your wishes, that's a story for a different day. Proper pre-arrangements can eliminate the burden of leaving a bill behind, the uncertainty of whether or not you will be taken care of after you have taken your last breath, and it can also eliminate so much stress on your grieving relatives left behind. It's another level of appreciation when a family comes in to make plans of final disposition and it's already done for them.

Come with me for a second.

Imagine everything being picked out. Casket, urn, flowers, programs, doves, location of service, cemetery, and any other items that would've made you feel complete; on top of that, from your diligent planning over the years and thinking ahead, everything is paid for!

MY GOSH!

Blissful thoughts if I must say so myself.

Alright so let's bring it back in.

I won't go into details and break down numbers because that simple math can be done at any point in time. If you do not specifically want to leave money to someone, you'll save yourself a great deal of money by choosing a local funeral home versus paying insurance premiums for the duration of your entire life. Work the figures on your own, if you don't believe me. The money will be set up as a trust fund and it'll be there for you whenever you need it. Well, you won't necessarily ever need it, but you get my drift.

This is not a conversation that most want to have, but I do feel it is necessary. As sure as we are living, we all have a date and time to leave this earth, so why not be completely ready. Spiritually, mentally, and physically; I am encouraging you to have that conversation so no family member is left clueless as to what would make you happy, and to eliminate confusion on opposing sides when it comes to making decisions for the final disposition. I don't like to make too many promises because things happen, but I am pretty much willing to bet my bottom dollar on this one.

HAVE THE CONVERSATION.

CHAPTER 9

NEAR DEATH EXPERIENCE

How close have you been?

Aside from the jellyfish incident that could've been potentially way worse than it was, I would consider myself to only have one really bad scare or near death experience.

In September of 2018, riding home after a regular day of work and stopping by a few stores, I merged onto the interstate on what had been such a great day. Minding my business, listening to my music, nothing out of the norm for me. The interstate is normally pretty busy when I get off, so I am always very cautious when it comes to driving home.

I WANT TO MAKE IT HOME SAFELY.

I'm always careful and as I always tell Granda, "I have to look out for myself and the other drivers too!" People are so careless when they're driving.   Between cell phones, music, tiredness, and simply just not being aware and paying attention to surroundings at any given moment, people are CARELESS. I've come to the conclusion that some people just never consider what may happen if they decide to drive however they are driving at the moment. Just because you are frustrated with traffic it doesn't mean you can just speed through and have your way. Move with traffic or just get off of the interstate. It can be so simple.

ANYWAY.

As I am traveling home to wind down for the day, this guy decides he wants to speed past the rest of the cars merging onto the interstate. I see him flying like a bat out of hell in my side mirror on the right. I'm thinking sure enough he's going to slow down because he clearly sees we are all coming up on more traffic, that's actually traveling slower than we are. Boy was I wrong! He continues to speed past the cars traveling East with us and even cuts off one car! Luckily, the car had enough space to slow down, but ultimately it didn't even matter much to them because he immediately switched lanes again. Only this time, he DID NOT have time or space to get over! Yea; he squeezed himself in anyway, and due to the space being small and traffic slowing down in front of him, he had to slam on his breaks abruptly.

Unfortunately, at this point I am the car that he has just cut off. I am the car that he did not have enough space to get over in front of. I am the car that he had to abruptly slow down in front of.

With him slowing down so fast in front of me, I was already slowing down as I was approaching the traffic up ahead, but I then had to press on my brakes even harder. As I press my brakes harder to try to avoid an accident, my wheels lock up and the car begins to fishtail down this busy interstate. I want to be pissed off so bad, but at this point I am like, "Oh my goodness, please do not let me hit anyone else!". I tried to keep my car as straight as possible, hoping "White Boy" would straighten up so that I would be able to fall back inline with the rest of the traffic. Well to my surprise, my car NEVER stopped fishtailing! At this point, I am fishtailing into a complete 180; my car is now facing the oncoming traffic. All I could do was grip my steering wheel, and in those few seconds I said, "Ok God, you got it from here". It was nothing else I could do, I felt completely helpless. Before that very moment, I had never felt so not-in-control and hands-off with a decision over my life. It's something you never want to feel.

TRUST ME.

Facing the oncoming traffic now, my car actually did not continue to drive forward, but it started going in reverse and up the hill backwards I went! Straight into the exit sign and I feel my car start to flip over!

realizing all motion has ceased

I start trying to get out of the car. In this moment, I do not know how certain things happen but I feel like the universe is always talking to me. I looked over to try to break my driver side window and all I see is Uncle Sam and Grandma Jessie looking at me. Grandma Jessie did not care for her picture to be taken so it was her praying hands.

Back home, the funeral home gives keepsakes to the family when a loved one passes and I keep them in my car, riding with me. My family is big, but very close, and we've always been taught to look out for each other so I figured, why not? Listen. I do not know how they got there from being placed in a little compartment in my car, but they were stuck in the window, side by side, facing me.

"WOW! Hello & Thank you!

I felt like seeing them gave me all the strength I needed in that moment to hold it all together and figure out how I was going to get out of the car. I did not know if the car would catch on fire or if I was close enough to an edge to fall over. I was completely blind to what was going on outside of my vehicle at this point. I knew I was close to the interstate because I could still hear cars, but it was pitch black. I tried to see if my door would budge. NOTHING. My driver side window was shattered, but would not break out because of the tint holding it together. A blessing and a curse because I did not have glass stuck in me everywhere, but it was also keeping me from getting out of this situation quickly. I looked to the passenger side window and tried to open that door because I figured it would be the same if I tried to break the window out. NOTHING. So I looked up, again; my car had flipped over and the front end was down towards the interstate. I looked up and saw the only window to shatter was the back window. I literally had to take my seatbelt off and stand straight up, crawl up to the window, and pull myself out of the car.

As I pulled myself up, I needed a second to completely grasp what had happened and to be thankful that I wasn't trapped in there, and also to see why I couldn't get my doors to open. Well, to my surprise, it was pitch black because that exit sign that I tore down... Yea... Well, it was laying over my car like a blanket. I wanted to have a reaction so bad but...

"OH MY GOD! OH MY GOD! ARE YOU OK? I SAW THE MAN CUT YOU OFF FROM THE START, AAAAAND HE ALSO KEPT DRIVING BUT I HAVE THE POLICE ON THE WAY ALREADY! I CALLED AS SOON AS YOUR CAR STARTED SPINNING! OH MY GOD, CAN I GIVE YOU A HUG? I AM SO GLAD YOU ARE OKAY!...WAIT YOU HAVEN'T BEEN DRINKING OR ANYTHING, HAVE YOU? THE POLICE ARE ALREADY ON THEIR WAY BUT I DO NOT WANT TO GET YOU IN ANY TROUBLE!", yells a sweet, hysterical lady with about three other people running back down the road towards me!

In a matter of seconds, and the first time I actually looked up and away from her... there were police cars and fire trucks and lights and sirens EVERYWHERE! I was so grateful but it was honestly overwhelming! I haven't had a clear second to even process everything that had taken place. I told her I was fine and thanked her for calling the police. I also thanked her for stopping for me and asked her to use the phone.

Knowing me in a situation like this and away from my family, I didn't want to call my mother or father because I did not want to freak them out, but I had no choice. My car is literally beside me upside down and going nowhere anytime soon. I called Daddy at work and as soon as I heard his voice, I BROKE! It hit me and I started crying as if it brought a reality to this situation that I am still here. I am still alive. I survived that terrible accident.

crying "Daddy, I don't know how I am even still alive, but I just wrecked and flipped my car!"

My daddy is cooler than the other side of the pillow, OK! I could hear the concern in his voice, but I could also feel him feeling my energy so of course, he remained calm to calm me. I appreciate the spirit of calmness that he has passed to me more than he could ever know. Part of the reason I was able to think through this accident happening; while simply not freaking out. Figure out what's next baby girl.

After that one phone call, I knew the word would spread like a wildfire to the rest of the immediate family. That wasn't really a good thing just yet though. My phone was still somewhere in my car and I am sure as people were calling and not getting an answer, they were wondering if I was ok and what was happening at the moment.

I was finally able to get my phone and check the calls and messages. To be honest, I didn't feel like calling a single person back but I knew everyone meant well, so I tried to respond to as many as I could. Every time a new police officer, firefighter, and whoever else was out there came up to me they all wanted to know what happened. I was exhausted from telling them and ready to go home. A paramedic came over and asked if I was sure I was the person in the car.

"I see you standing here, but by the looks of that car over there, I'm not exactly sure how you are standing here... untouched.", says the paramedic as he approached me, asked questions and checked my limbs, chest, and head to make sure I didn't need to be rushed off before everything was in place at the scene. He told me he needed me to come to the ambulance so he could check my blood pressure and temperature, so I walked over with him. As he goes to get in the ambulance, he asked me if I could step up in the ambulance with him. I stopped, looked up at him, and smiled.

"Sir, with all due respect I know you are doing you job, but I am a mortician and after that accident, I most certainly do not want to sit on a stretcher. Let's skip that part because it's obviously not my turn right now. If I come up, I will only sit on the side with you."

He laughed and agreed to allow me to sit on the side.

As he was checking my body and asking me questions, he said he was so surprised that I didn't black out or anything, but he was most certainly glad I was looking and feeling fine. Good talks and good laughs and on to the next part... All while looking out of the back of the ambulance at my baby over there completely broken up. I've had that car for 9 years with not one single problem. In fact, after 9 years, I had just recently put a new battery in it. Not to mention, the jerk drove off in the midst of seeing all of this unfold. I know he knew he cut me off, and I'm sure he looked back in his mirror and saw my car fishtailing. But... Bless his heart.

Now that I've been throughly checked out and drilled on a "heap" of questions, as Granda would say, I'm heading back to the side of the road to wait on the tow truck to flip my car over so I can get my phone. My Apple watch was blowing up .

Firefighter: Baby, I really hate that you were even in this accident but I am so glad you took that exit sign down. Do you know what's up a little higher from where your car flipped?

Me: *looks up and then at the firefighter*

Firefighter: NOTHING. It's a ledge. If you didn't hit the sign and your car kept going, it wouldn't have been anything else there to help you stop. That's a blessing there.

Me: OH, WOW!

All I could do was shake my head and smile.

My car was now upright and I was able to get my phone as well as some other items before it was taken away.

Mommy called and let me say that she is nowhere near as calm as Daddy, so I already knew how this call to her baby girl was going to be. She was antsy, nervous, on edge, and wanted to be here with me. To me, normal motherly instincts to run to her baby's rescue. She had a year of going through a mastectomy, chemotherapy, and radiation. She had not been released to drive yet. I told her I was fine and heading home. I told her not to get on the road that late, and just to wait until the morning.

Guess who pulls up in about two and half hours, when it probably takes a good three and a half to four hours to get to me...

shaking my head

Mommy had pulled up. At my door after I specifically told her to wait until morning. I fussed at her so bad because I didn't know what I would've done if something was to happen to her on that dark, busy road that late at night. I had no car to get to her, I just could not.

Nonetheless, I'm grateful for her. Her strength is amazing. She admires my strength, but I think she underestimates the source that passed it on. I fussed but I was glad to see her face, just as I was glad to hear Daddy's voice on the phone. I needed someone there and she came through for me that night. After a long evening, we sat around and talked, laughed, and I didn't have to deal with the night alone. My girl.

That night closed out, I said my prayers and I went to sleep.

Now... The days to come.

That night outside and in the ambulance… all of the questions that were asked. I was wondering, why do they do this in the moment of an accident? Adrenaline is rushing and it's in the heat of the moment.

Does anyone really have time to think about whether something is really hurting them, when it's not obvious like a broken bone?

The next three weeks were worse than the beginnings of my collegiate volleyball seasons, when Coach Kohn and Zack would be getting us whipped into shape. Those were some intense workouts, and I'm sure my fellow athletes out there understand getting back in shape for a new season. New muscles being used and worked out; soreness literally EVERYWHERE! I felt like someone had beaten me up and left me on the side of the road. I could barely walk some days, but I didn't complain once because I was still here. Still here to tell my story. I continued to go to work everyday. Some days better than others, but all of them were really painful days. Meeting with families, consoling families, and in the most pain I had ever felt in my life. But I made it through.

Thank goodness.

I MADE IT THROUGH.

CHAPTER 10

NURSING HOME NEGLIGENCE

Bedsore: an ulceration of tissue deprived of adequate blood supply by prolonged pressure.

Nursing homes and assisted living facilities are there to help our loved ones in their time of need when we are unable to do all of the work ourselves.

What breaks my heart here is seeing family members, who allow the ones they say they love the most to be admitted into these facilities and never check on their well-being. When someone is checked into these facilities, it does not mean you should let them be and hope everything will be taken care of. It means they are there for assistance, but you should still do everything possible to make sure they are being taken care of, just as they would do for themselves if they could. This applies when you're present with them but from afar as well.

There are so many elderly clients and/or disabled clients that come in with bed sores on their buttocks, back, hips, elbows, and heels. This does not happen from simply not feeling well, bedsores are a result of negligence. If a person is not able to move around themselves while they are in bed, they will need to be turned into different positions every so often in order to prevent this. We cannot always depend on the facilities to know and also do what is necessary, but every time you are able to physically visit your loved one, you can do your part by making sure these things are not happening. If they are on their back every time you come in, ask them if they are feeling any irritation in or on their backs. They may feel it, but if it has been too long, they may not. You should still roll them a little to check it out. Some favor a certain side or position once their mobility has been effected, but the same techniques apply. Make sure they are not on the same side or in the same position every single time you come in. I cannot stress this enough. Even if they cannot talk and tell you exactly what is going on, be their voice for them. Massage their limbs, rub their feet, whatever you can do to help the circulation continue to flow properly. Exercise is good for blood flow while we are healthy enough to still be mobile, but it is also important in cases where we are not able to move around as much.

I sit at work and listen to families preach about how much they loved their mother, father, sister, uncle, cousin, etc.; then I get in the back and they have a bedsore so deep on their buttocks that the entire hip bone is exposed.

HOW?

WHY?

HOW DO YOU LET SOMEONE YOU LOVE END UP LIKE THIS?

By the way, this is not just a hypothetical situation, this is a real-life example.

Take a second to imagine how you would feel living with a bedsore on your butt so deep and so bad that your bone is showing, out in the open, clear...

Partially ignorant to how the body functions and what happens when blood is not circulating as it should, but sometimes a person is vocal, and they would just rather let the nurses pack the wound instead of tending to the issue. The person with the hip bone exposed had been in that position long enough for the blood flow to be nonexistent in that area and become necrotic. At this point, the flesh is dead and would begin to stink if not cleaned and properly packed. You would begin to think there was a dead animal in the room. None of us like when we have forgotten about some food that we tossed in the trashcan and begins to spoil in our kitchen, so I am certain our loved ones do not appreciate sitting in a bedsore that smells bad enough to make them nauseous on top of the illness they are already dealing with.

It was sickening to see, and to think of how the love for them was just cowardly professed in my office.

I've seen elbows and heels that were never lifted off of the bed and now look as though gangrene has settled in very well. Can you even imagine having a sore on your elbow?! I've seen bedsores on backs of heavier individuals and yes, you guessed it... the thought of lifting a heavy person to make sure this is not happening, is the last thing on someone's mind because it's more work. When this happens, the next issue is the odor coming from the bedsore that gets stuck in your nose and seems like there's no escaping it. Of course the family is wondering what the smell is. It would be so easy to help and make them acknowledge the fact they know exactly what it is, but here is where you have to keep it professional.

Nothing personal, business is business.

Admitting our parents, grandparents, siblings, and really anybody we love into a nursing home is a really tough situation. If you are ever in this predicament where you or someone you know has to make this decision, please check on your loved one. Make sure they are being turned every hour or so. Make sure they are getting the massages they need to keep their blood flowing. Make sure they are simply, but heavily, getting that much needed attention. I have a deep appreciation for the nurses that pay attention and make it happen.

CHAPTER 11

WORKPLACE CHALLENGES

Youngest.
Least respected.
Over looked.

Maybe not all, but many of us know the struggle of finding a job especially something available in your field of study, which you look forward to actually making a career out of.

When I was younger, the thoughts of working a job were pretty interesting to me. I thought it was so cool how cashiers would scan all of the items so fast, as we heard the beep come from the register.

"BEEP...BEEP...BEEP...BEEP....BEEP..."

The innocence of a child.

I absolutely loved it. It's so funny to me now and as many would say today, it was one of those noises that was awkwardly satisfying. My brother and I would go to the grocery store with my grandparents to get our usual groceries for the house and it never failed. Every time we came in the house they would sit the groceries on the table for us to do our thing! Haha! We would take turns scanning the items and then pass them down the line so the other person could put the item away. Oh yea, don't forget that beep that I loved; we made our own beeping noises. There was so much work on some days, that we considered fun, but I'm more than sure our grandparents did not mind one bit!

Thankfully, it was not mandatory or necessary for me to lock down a job at a young age. I am grateful in so many ways for this not being the lifestyle I had to experience early in life, but I extend much respect and gratitude to those of you who did. Daddy always said school work and sports were our jobs and that was just what we focused on.

Entering the working world was difficult. When I first moved, I didn't have a job for over a year and it was really hard. Thoughts of applying for entry level jobs weighed heavy on my mind, but it's crazy when you go to apply and they already have all of these requirements. Is this really considered entry level? I've never gone on a job and they didn't have some form of on-the-job training so why are your requiring certain things for an entry level position?
Make it make sense, please.
I was finally able to land a job and worked there, until I was asked if I was interested in working at a funeral home. What a

blessing that was because that job did exactly what I needed it to do, but it was not where I wanted to be, which made it harder and harder as time went by to actually want to be there. I really pray for you reading this and everyone to find love in their career, as well as their environment because that plays a huge part too.

Working at the funeral home allowed me to learn the ins and outs and slowly grasp onto different duties. One thing I can always tell you for sure is that no two days are alike around here. Every day is a new day with new happenings. There was an older lady working with me when I first started. Everyone was used to her answering the phones and helping them with anything they needed at the time; people like to deal with who they know. It was not always easy to get people to understand that I could provide the assistance they needed. The manager would tell them, my coworkers would tell them and I would even try to assure them I was capable, but that was a dud. People would call on the phone and ask for this lady even if I told them she was busy at the moment. They would rather wait for hours. I know this sounds crazy because you would think they would be able to see in-person that I am capable of helping them, or even over the phone by listening to see if I sound sure of what I am discussing with them. However, the reality here is the fact that I had three things working against me at this point. I was the new person, I looked like I could still be in grade school (with a small stature) and my voice was soft. It just wasn't what the clients wanted to accept at the time, and I understood. I gave them time and I hung in there, because I knew eventually the tables would turn and everyone would love to see me coming to help them, or to hear my voice on the phone.

I specifically remember this one lady that came in and I was the only one working in the office on this particular day, so I stood up from my desk and went to the door to greet her.

"Hello, how may I help you?"

The lady acts as if she didn't even hear me and tried to walk over me in the door, looking over my head and into the office behind me. I politely stepped to the side and let her have a look like I was totally clueless as to what she was doing.

"Are you looking for someone?"

She goes on to say she needs help with some prices and possibly making arrangements for one of her family members.

"Ok, well I'm here trying to help you. There's no one else here at the moment."

She looks and asks me how old I am, with her brows raised. In my head, I'm thinking about how disrespectful she is being right now and doesn't even care, and why I would be the only one here if I was not capable of helping you. People really do not think logically, and I love to share with others that common sense is not too common, unfortunately. I avoided her question about my age simply because it was none of her business and she was out of place for asking me this when she was obviously here for other reasons. I gave her the prices and information that she needed, answered all of her questions about our services and what we would be able to provide for her, told her the legal steps that had to be taken for us to pick up or receive remains, and I mean… I gave her all of the little, tiny details. I had to lay it all out for her and juice it up really nice, so that she knew when she called or came back in, I knew exactly what I was talking about and at that moment, I knew no one could've done it better.

As she was leaving, she thanked me for helping her and giving her details about what needed to be done, because this was her first time having to actually handle arranging a funeral herself. I'm sure you're wondering if she ever offered up an apology, because I was waiting too. Naw. Just kidding, most of the time these kinds of people do not come with apologies for what they've done and it's understood; not right, but I understand and that was fine with me. As long as she left my office with more knowledge than she came in with, it was good in my book. She'll probably also think twice about underestimating someone because of how young they look now. No apology, but she commended me on "knowing my stuff". It works for me.

Good day lady.

That wasn't just on one occasion. It happens all the time and still happens every now and then, 6 years later. It is what it is. I do my part and let that change their mind, whether they acknowledge it or not. I just know once they leave my office, they never call back asking for someone else. They call asking for Janae'. It feels good to know they have confidence in me providing the accurate information they need, it just takes some a little time to warm up. I'm like that outside of work so I choose not be biased while working.

CHAPTER 12

CORONAVIRUS
"COVID-19"

Let's jump right in here to why funeral service workers are not considered front line workers or essential workers. Does it make sense to you because it does not make sense to me or sit well with me. I have listened to people complain about working from home and not being able to go into the office and on the flip side praising all doctors, nurses, etc but we have not been able to skip a day.

As we all know, people have not stopped dying due to Covid-19, more have passed. So what happens when they pass away and who's next in line to deal with the spread of the virus. Not only do we have to deal with the infected remains but we also have to invite the families into our office to make arrangements not knowing for sure if they have the virus or not. We've had to adjust our office rules to accommodate families. We've had to listen to them complain and give us attitudes because they cannot bring their entire family in to make funeral arrangements. We've had to deal with attitudes because we were not allowed to have services at one point with more than the immediate family present. When the rules were lifted a little, then the complaints were about why only a certain number of people could attend the services. We started off at like ten people which eventually went to thirty. Not much, but better than not having a service at all if you ask me. Attitudes about not wanting to wear masks because they are not sick. Attitudes about not being able to just sit around in the building, socializing; we simply asked them to respect the immediate family so they would have enough time to spend with their loved one without having to go in and out all day. Of course we all know funerals serve as mini family reunions and we respect that but right now we have a deeper issue to try to control. We've held a lady for a month because her daughters wanted to wait until the virus passed. One of them didn't want to bury their mother without having a service. She didn't want her mother's service to only have ten people. Nothing was working for her and COVID did not matter to her, she wanted what she wanted. Every week it was something different until I told them they had to go ahead and make a decision because the rules were not changing any time soon. Patience was at an all-time high but soon it was going to turn into a question of how her mom was going to look in the casket after being there for so long. To eliminate that, we made it decision making time.

Wear your mask.

My statements at the beginning of this chapter were not to discredit anyone in the medical field because I know they work hard and anyone that has had to work through this COVID madness knows how rough it's been. I have actually gained a new appreciation and truly commend doctors for always having to work with masks on; especially surgeons. They make life changing decisions while working behind a mask. AMAZING!

I have been faithfully wearing my mask but I have also been faithfully having headaches and exhausted from struggling to talk through them all day. When you don't naturally have a voice that projects it can seem muffled talking with a mask on which makes you feel like you have to scream. Not literally, but to know me is to know how soft my voice can be. My mom used to fuss about me not talking loud enough but apparently I get it from my daddy. Other than the headaches from speaking loudly, they are also coming from not being able to drink enough water throughout the day. Normally I would be able to talk and get a sip here and there but now with my mouth covered I try to make sure I keep my mask up so the families will feel comfortable. Honestly, most of the time I don't even think about drinking water because I know my mouth is covered. It sucks and I know my body pretty well to know it drains me when I haven't had enough water especially when I am having a busy day. When I feel myself getting sluggish and weak, I realize I haven't had my water for the day. I've had plenty restless nights and by the time I fall asleep it feels like it's time to get back up and do it all over again.Waking up thinking, "Just a few more minutes, please!!!"

Cleaning.

Let me start by saying it tickled my soul and I was kind of disappointed when the virus went crazy and people were buying all of the cleaning supplies out of the stores. I mean I want everybody to clean and be safe but I was stuck wondering what everyone was doing before this. Were hands and houses not being cleaned. I've heard people say they've never washed their hands so much in their lives. Meanwhile, I've always washed my hands a million times a day and prefer soap and water over sanitizer. Well the simple fact here is some people are naturally nasty. They do not properly wash their hands. They do not clean their houses thoroughly. They do not care about germs on the regular when everything is "going right". It's unbelievable. I am happy to say Mommy has been cleaning thoroughly, keeping Lysol, bleach, and other disinfectants in the house since forever. As I got older I made sure to do the same so in this case I did not have to rush out to the stores in all of the chaos. I had plenty of everything that I needed already in house. I was also glad I didn't have to settle for buying a $20 can of Lysol on Amazon. Those prices were getting outrageous while all of the stores were sold out. The back and forth about whether or not the virus lasts on surfaces was also unsettling. One minute it was said that the virus was easily being passed on surfaces and then it was changed to say that it wasn't. It makes you think about the series of events taking place. People breaking their necks to find products to keep surfaces clean just for the media to say it no longer lasts on surfaces. The money has been spent and the companies have made bank at this point. But, better safe than sorry right?

Uncertainty of Exposure.

      I won't call any companies out here but they released information out to funeral homes that was extremely contradicting. At first they were saying they weren't sure if the virus dies when a person dies but we should use normal PPE and precautions. Next they said it dies after about 3 hours and don't quote me on this but it changed to like 6-8 hours or so but the bottom line here is that it was a lot of back and forth and we didn't really know what to believe about this new strand of COVID. Do I want to touch the bodies right now? Being transparent here, normally once cases that are not infectious have been cleaned, disinfected, and embalmed I don't always wear gloves for certain things like when I am setting facial features, putting on eyelashes, and some of the small tasks. Gloves don't allow you to really feel everything and get as close to the features as you need to. Ungloved hands work best for me in certain situations and when I can I will take them off. Before you frown your face up remember that we are talking about people and not walking diseases. It's the same as someone touching you while you're alive or you touching someone alive; the person just no longer has any breath.
      In this case even if a body was considered to be non-infectious I've still only felt comfortable with having my

gloves on because the hospitals here have not been on top of things when it comes to discharge papers and letting the funeral homes know if it was a COVID case or not. I actually had a few families come in for a person that was said to be COVID negative and the family tells us their loved one had tested positive or they were tested because of symptoms but their results had not come back yet. Crazy, right? We've had families come in saying their loved ones were fine in facilities and then all of a sudden they are diagnosed with COVID and then the next day they were on a respirator. It makes the whole situation scary. Are these people really dying from coronavirus? That's a conversation for a different day and I am not even discussing it here. Let's just say it's been a bumpy road down this journey of figuring COVID deaths out. Some that have been said to die from this virus don't even have Coronavirus on their death certificate. Make it make sense here because I am flabbergasted by even the thought of this being possible. It's not a good look and doesn't help families have closure when the only thing they have been told is that their loved one died from COVID.

To this day COVID is still real and happening but the cases have definitely slowed down a little. Families still complain about the number of people that can be at services and still want to make the rules; but in the midst of all of the difficult clients you have the blessings that pass through that understand and appreciate the precautions that we are taking in our establishment. I really appreciate them; more than they'll ever know. I thank them all the time for simply not giving us a hard time about something that is out of any of our control.

One day I hope the world sees, acknowledges, and respects the funeral service industry a lot more. We go above and beyond to help families have a beautiful, lasting images of their loved ones and it pretty much goes unnoticed. I feel its partially because nobody wants to discuss death but funerals should be looked at as a celebration of life instead of a dark moment that could possibly haunt you like your worst nightmare. I'm one voice speaking up to make a change in this area and even if I do not continue to work in a funeral home directly, I will continue in this line of work sharing knowledge and helping to put a better image about death and dying in every individual's mind that I can reach. I encourage you to do the same. Speak up! This is an interesting career path and it's certainly not for everyone but someone has to do it to allow all of us to properly celebrate our family members that we love dearly.

Rant Over.

CHAPTER 13
JESSIE ROAD

Jessie is my paternal grandmother. One of the three that I was blessed to know and experience life with. I had a very unique relationship with Grandma Jessie from a young age due to the huge age gap and difference in times from when she was growing up and when I was growing up but it was all love. I grew up to understand it all; why certain things were ok at my parents house was not ok at hers and I am grateful for the lessons learned.

Grandma Jessie passed in 2011 and just as Grandma Celia Mae left an imprint on my life in 2000, she left one too when it comes to the death and dying world. The dying process is hard to deal with because as humans we do not want to let go but when you have the chance to experience the process with a loved one, it can be very gratifying. Aside from disease and traumatic endings, you learn death does not hurt. You can literally witness the peacefulness of someone dying if you are able to control the heavy emotions during this time.

It only hurts the ones left behind.

Grandma Jessie was admitted to hospice; one of the hardest days and worst set of words to hear during that time. Once you're in hospice care it is all about comfort until you take your last breath. It's the reality of knowing the days are limited at this point; any day could be the last. It's the time you get to show your love again just in case you feel like you haven't done enough. It is not a time to be scared but a time to be appreciative for all of the life that you were able to share with that particular person. It is time to lay it all out on the line. It is time to… RELEASE!

Let it all go in preparation of letting someone go.

I cannot remember exactly how long Grandma was in hospice but I remember Daddy telling me she was asking about me and I had to make sure I got there to see her. I couldn't imagine her taking her last breath without being in her presence one more time. I do believe when we are on our way out we wait on certain people and certain things before we decided all is well and drift off into our forever homes; whatever that may be for you personally. I drove to South Carolina that night and went to see her on the next day. She was lying in bed; still, but happy to see me. "Hey there, what are you doing here?", she said as she looked my way smiling. It warmed my heart. Days went by and we made several visits. While I was there, everything I ate she wanted some; spaghetti, ice cream, apple juice, you name it. She was no longer on medication at this time and it seemed like her skin and face was looking younger by the day. Her hair was always pretty and soft but it seemed to be getting thickervery day. She always liked for me to comb and braid her hair so I was happy to do it one last time while I was there. Mommy rubbed her feet some days and everyone made sure they turned her because she wasn't mobile anymore; it was sad to see life leaving her body. Daddy and his siblings were taking turns staying the night with her and this particular night he was unsure of who was staying so I volunteered. No need to ask around, I'm here and I'll stay. I don't mind at all.

My brother found out I was staying the night at the hospital and said he would stay with me. Due to seeing signs of Grandma Jessie over the previous days, I knew at any moment now dramatic changes could happen. She had already stopped eating almost completely at this point and her breathing was inconsistent. I talked to my brother to make sure he understood what could happen during these final days and he said he would be fine so...

Let the night begin!

It started off as a night of watching television and we were doing something on my computer as she rested. She called my name so I went to the bed to see what she needed and she reached out for my hand. She didn't really want or need anything; well I guess she did because she wanted to hold my hand. I stood there holding her hand for what seemed like the longest time. I actually thought she fell asleep and tried to move my hand but she squeezed it a little harder. Seeing that she was not sleep and could still feel me, I asked my brother to bring a chair over so I could sit beside her while I held her hand. Sitting there, holding her hand on the bed I began watching television again. Maybe twenty or thirty minutes had gone by and all of a sudden Grandma's right hand shoots up in the air along with a death rattle that shocked both of us. I always heard and read about a death rattle but to experience one was different. Trying to be still enough to not scare her, I looked back to make sure my brother was ok and he was ready to do something to help. I calmly told him it was ok and she's fine; we just have to let these things play out naturally. He looked scared but he seemed sure of what I told him. She peacefully rested her right arm again and the rattle slowly faded away. She mumbled words that we could not make out but never really seemed to wake up in that moment. Here we are having a whole moment of tranquil transitioning while she holds my hand for comfort. A moment that could never be forgotten even if one tried their hardest. To this day; 9 years later, I've kept this moment to myself aside from sharing the night with my parents and my brother. It was special and I thank her for it. I am glad she did not leave us in that moment but it seemed like it was no more than two days later and she decided to let go and take her final rest.

Harsh reality with a sense of certainty and belief that she was at peace and ready to rest; completely.

Grandma Jessie lived on Jessie Road in real life and the good times we've had as a family on Jessie Road are countless. She was the backbone, the glue that kept everyone together. She was the matriarch. Powerful, funny, quiet but did not mind saying what needed to be said. Her food was ALWAYS amazing and never lacking the love necessary for making a good, hearty dinner. Her fried chicken was superb and no one could make it like her except my Uncle Skipper. I have not had a sweet potato pie as perfect, delicate, and evenly strained since she left us. When she cooked you would think her pots were automatically seasoned because she never missed in the kitchen. I started at an early age helping her make fruit cakes for the entire family and I am so glad I did. Daddy and I would help her and as she got older, we took over to keep the fruit cake tradition going. It has only been us since 2011 and every year the question of the season is, "Am I going to get my fruit cake this year?". A lot goes into our fruit cakes and honestly I am not even a fan because of all of the fruits and nuts but I will say our cakes are pretty amazing. I hope to one day have children of my own to help us and continue on for generations to come. Some traditions should never end. I hope the fruit cake traditions last to infinity and I pray the story of where they started lasts just as long. This will be a reminder of when, what, how, and who for years to come.

To Grandma Jessie:

I loved you. I loved your house. I still love sitting in your rocking chair, looking out towards the field of dirt that is now covered with trees. I appreciate your chicken coop and the laughs I get from growing up thinking only brown eggs were real chicken eggs. I have the same love for coffee and Pepsi that you had. I love cooking. I love baking and still make fruit cakes for the family every year. They love them. I look forward to nurturing my children. And building a tight knit family as you've done with your nine. You've given an example of how it should be. Many have left us, but our family is still growing! Without you, there would be no us. We are grateful and you are unquestionably missed.

Last but not least; thank you for welcoming me on your journey and taking me down Jessie Road one last time. The last time was very personal. I wish it didn't have to end, but I am appreciative for the comfort you left me with and I am not afraid or worried.

ALL IS WELL.

CHAPTER 14

SHARE YOUR LIGHT IN A DARK WORLD

I've always wanted others to feel good and loved since I was younger but the older I get the more I really try to keep this way of life up. I hate to think someone is sad, upset, or feeling any negative way because of me.

While working I have realized how many people are in dark spaces but do not realize how bad it is. Some are aware but don't have anyone to confide in. Some are angry and project their anger in different ways on other people that have absolutely nothing to do with what's going on in their world. Some think everybody should be in a funk because they are.

I've had plenty days of being in a position where I literally serve as a counselor all day, back to back, person after person, situation after situation and honestly it's exhausting but to know and see someone leave my office in a different space and ten times lighter makes it all worth it. I really hate to take days off from work and I don't even take sick days because I see everyday as an opportunity to help someone in some way.

If I woke up not having the best day, not long after I get to work something always happens to lift my mood! It never fails. It's like the universe offers me the perfect balance; an equal exchange of energy for my faithfulness to my clients!

My clients never know what kind of day I'm having but if I know it has not been the best I try to always make sure I thank them and let them know how much I've appreciated their energy on that particular day. This career I have chosen is a lot and it is a lot I have to do by myself on the daily. I get tired but I cannot just fail my clients by not showing up and not trying my hardest to give them my best everyday. They need me to be that strength for them on that particular day. They need my words of encouragement. They need my little powerful hugs. They need my friendly face and kindness. They need that ear to listen to all of their problems and why it feels like the weight of the world is on their shoulders. They need that extra push towards the light at the end of the tunnel. They need my guidance and words of wisdom. Old and young, mean or nice, I can provide at least one thing that my clients need; often times way more.

In my six years in the funeral industry, I've grown to love strangers more than I could ever imagine I would. They love me like I'm a part of their family. I meet with them and help them plan services for their family and when we are done with business they come back to visit me. Some bring cards, some bring food, some just bring hugs, laughs, and words of appreciation. They leave knowing that my door is always open to them and don't mind taking advantage of that opportunity. My clients have allowed and helped me to grow as a person on a mental and spiritual level. They've helped me grow on a business level as well because you can never gain too much knowledge about how to treat people, how to handle situations; good and bad, or how every person you deal with in life will be different. I've learned there's good in everyone. Everybody has a soft spot, you just have to be open to allowing them to be themselves. Practice patience with "difficult" or "mean" individuals and watch how things change for your relationship with them.

I had a client that was paying on his pre-arrangements and his wife's pre-arrangements. At one point they would come together but after awhile she stopped coming and he would come alone. I asked about her and he said she was slowly forgetting things and would be having good days and bad days; sweetest lady ever. He came in one day and got home confused about his payment. I was patient and explained to him several times but he just wasn't getting it. He got so frustrated and told me I was wrong and tried to explain why and eventually got off the phone, still confused but convinced he was right and that I just wasn't understanding him. About an hour later on the same day, he called back apologizing because he finally realized what I was telling him and how I was trying to save him some money in the long run. He apologized over and over; apologized until the day he left. He would come by with his I Love Jesus hat on to make his payments faithfully and we were able to laugh about the situation but he was sure to remind me of how bad he felt for getting frustrated with me that day. He was always a pleasant face to see and I was sad to see him go but it was a pleasure to literally serve him until the end. I was able to meet his relatives and share our story. I miss our talks. He would always leave the office saying " I love you a bushel and a peck and a hug around the neck!" I pray he's resting well.

One of my other buddies would come by to make payments or if he saw I didn't have anyone in the office he would just come in to talk for a while before he walked home. When he would drive, he would ride by and wave. He was so sweet and always had some jokes for me. Over time he slowly started coming by less than he normally would and it turned out he had been in the hospital. Unfortunately, it started a pattern of being in and out of the hospital but whenever he was feeling strong enough to get out he would always come by to see me. He told me he wasn't doing well but he was hanging in there. I watched his health deteriorate day by day; week by week until I was eventually talking to him one last time in the casket his family chose for him.

I don't know most of the people I work on personally but when you know one you always wonder why they had to leave. Fortunately when one's time has expired, another comes to bring some new light. New person, new personality, new situations, new conversations, new non-judgmental bonds. I cherish and love every single one. We create bonds and build relationships with others and it doesn't mean I have to know every single detail but sharing certain aspects of your life can be a great help to someone whether they speak on it or not. Tear down the walls and be free. Be open to love and laughter. Be open to listening to others even when you may not be having the best day. Be open to sharing your personal experiences, positive and negative. Make the best out of every situation. Live freely. Love unconditionally. Give willingly. Most importantly, don't forget to share your light in a dark world.

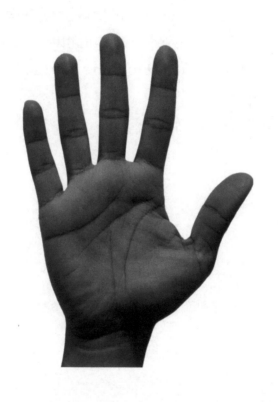